The No-Homework Women's Bible Study: Group Hug

D0369516

By CHRISTINE TATE

This book belongs to: _____

The No-Homework Women's Bible Study: Group Hug

By Christine Tate

Copyright © 2013 Christine Tate, Copyright © 2020 Christine Tate Revised and Expanded Edition

ISBN-13: 978-1482083910

DEDICATION

This book is dedicated to my parents, without whom I would not be the person I am today. To my mother, Nancy Holowenko, a woman of strong Christian faith who nurtured me in my walk with the Lord, I thank you for the guidance you gave me. To my father, Richard Holowenko, a man of strong direction, I thank you for showing me what it means to single-mindedly pursue your goals. I love you, Mom and Dad.

I would also like to thank the Women's Bible Study group at NAS Oceana Chapel for helping me "test drive" this study. You are a great group of women and I truly value your friendship and support!

CONTENTS

GROUP CONTACT INFORMATION

NAME	PHONE	EMAIL

USING THIS STUDY GUIDE

"Not forsaking the assembling of ourselves together, as the manner of some is; but encouraging one another: and so much more, as you see the day coming." Hebrews 10:25

The study group should be a safe, loving, supportive environment to explore various topics as God guides you through the power of the Holy Spirit. Before beginning this study, please make sure all group members are aware of and follow these ground rules:

- o   What is shared in the group, stays in the group!

- o   Be a good listener and an even better Christian sister.

- o   Be patient, kind, loving, and respectful of other group members.

- o   Always give godly, biblically sound advice that is rooted in scripture.

At the first meeting, everyone should pass their book around the circle and write their contact information in each group member's book using the page provided at the beginning of the book. This series involves passing books around from time to time and this will help books get back to their proper owners.

It is helpful to choose a group leader to keep things on track and moving forward. Each weekly study begins with an **Opening Prayer.** After leading the group through the prayer, the leader should introduce the **Ice Breaker** activity coordinating the activity so that everyone has a chance to participate and share their responses. Then, moving on to the **Lesson** which includes **God's Promise**, the **Weekly Word Study**, and **Scripture**, take turns reading each section as you go around the circle. Next, the group leader reads the **Commentary** and then guides the group through the **Discussion Questions**. The questions are designed to stimulate group interaction—tangents are encouraged! To wrap up the discussion, the leader should read the **Weekly Challenges** section to the group. The **Weekly Challenges** are optional suggestions for group members to try during the week to extend the discussion into action. To close the session, the group leader should first ask if there are any prayer requests within the group, then lead everyone in the **Closing Prayer** given at the end of the weekly lesson. Be sure to write down specific prayer needs for group members and notes for personal growth in the space provided at the end of the weekly lesson on the **Notes** page. A suggestion to encourage group bonding is for everyone to stand arm-in-arm in a circle for a "group hug" during the closing prayer.

If you enjoy this study and would like to find other studies written by Christine Tate or be notified when new studies become available, please visit http://christinetate.webstarts.com. In addition, Christine Tate has a blog at http://christinetate.wordpress.com. Feedback is encouraged as I always love to hear from my Christian sisters.

May God bless you, guide you and nurture you as you begin this journey!

AVAILABLE TITLES

The No-Homework Women's Bible Study: Group Hug

The No-Homework Women's Bible Study: Group Hug II

The No-Homework Women's Bible Study: Group Hug III

The No-Homework Women's Bible Study: Group Hug IV

The No-Homework Women's Bible Study: Group Hug V

The No-Homework Women's Bible Study: Group Hug VI

The No-Homework Women's Bible Study: Group Hug VII

The No-Homework Women's Bible Study: Group Hug Holidays

The No-Homework Women's Bible Study: Group Hug Marriage

Are We the Terminal Generation?

My Prayer Journal: Remembering God's Answers

AVAILABLE IN LARGE PRINT

The No-Homework Women's Bible Study: Group Hug

COMING SOON!

The No-Homework Women's Bible Study: Group Hug VIII

The No-Homework Women's Bible Study: Group Hug Hot Topics

A Christian's Devotional for Surviving Divorce

Independence in the Suburbs

WEEK 1: TAKING CARE OF YOURSELF

Opening Prayer *(5 minutes)*: Lord, we thank You for this time together to grow deeper in our walk with You and our fellowship with each other. We humbly ask You to open our hearts and minds as we receive Your word that it may yield fruit in our lives, deepen our knowledge of You and strengthen our family bonds as children in Your eternal kingdom. May we receive Your favor and blessing upon us as we strive to love more deeply, live godlier lives and become more like You with each passing day. In Jesus' name we pray, Amen.

Ice Breaker *(10 minutes)*: Have everyone take five minutes to fill out the questionnaire below. When everyone is done, group members should pass their book to the person on their right. Go around the room and have each person introduce the person whose book they are holding. After everyone has had a chance to introduce someone, return all the books to the correct person.

My name is: _____

An interesting fact about me is:

_____

A nickname I have/had is: _____

My favorite hobby is: _____

My biggest fear is: _____

My favorite movie is: _____

If I could live anywhere in the world, it would be: _____

Lesson *(10 minutes)*:

God's Promise: God knows our needs even before we do and has promised to fulfill those needs.

Weekly Word Study

[7] And when you pray, do not use vain **repetitions**... *Matt. 6:7*

BATTOLOGEO (pronounced bat-tol-og-eh'-o): Repetitious prayer refers to the act of either repeating the same phrase over and over or adding extra, unnecessary words to a prayer. It is believed that the Greek word "battologeo" connects back to a famous stutterer named Battus who was the King of Cyrene. History also presents another person by the name of Battus who wrote excessively wordy and tedious poems. In either case, this verse indicates that God prefers simple, to-the-point, straightforward conversation with us expressed in a genuine, heartfelt manner. When you take your needs to the Lord in prayer, always bare your soul with sincerity and reveal your innermost, private thoughts to Him.

Scripture:

GOD KNOWS OUR NEEDS

[7] And when you pray, do not use vain repetitions as the heathen do. For they think that they will be heard for their many words. [8] Therefore do not be like them. For your Father knows the things you have need of before you ask Him. *Matthew 6:7-8*

GOD VALUES US

[29] Are not two sparrows sold for a copper coin? And not one of them falls to the ground apart from your Father's will. [30] But the very hairs of your head are all numbered. [31] Do not fear therefore; you are of more value than many sparrows. *Matthew 10:29-31*

GOD'S ABILITY TO MEET OUR NEEDS

[19] And my God shall supply all your need according to His riches in glory by Christ Jesus. *Philippians 4:19*

GOD EXPECTS US TO TAKE CARE OF OURSELVES TOO

[42] Or how can you say to your brother, "Brother, let me remove the speck that is in your eye," when you yourself do not see the plank that is in your own eye? Hypocrite! First remove the plank from your own eye, and then you will see clearly to remove the speck that is in your brother's eye. *Luke 6:42*

Commentary: In order to be the best wife, mother, daughter, sister, friend, co-worker and neighbor that we can be, we have to first take care of ourselves.   But, before you can take care of yourself, it is necessary to be able to identify your unique physical, mental, emotional and spiritual needs. Only then can you find the balance you deserve in your life. With the constant chatter and distractions surrounding women in their daily lives, sometimes it can be hard to identify what those needs are specifically. Have faith that even when life runs you around in circles, God is still in control, knows your needs and will meet those needs whenever, wherever and however they present. Above all, remember, you matter to God.

Discussion Questions *(30 minutes)*:

1. What are your current needs (physical, mental, emotional and spiritual)? Are those needs effectively being met?

2. What steps can you take to meet those needs yourself? What role does God play in meeting those needs?

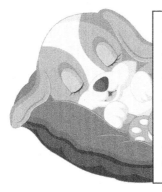

> *A Gallup poll states that Americans average 6.8 hours of sleep at night. This number has been declining since 1942 when the average person enjoyed 7.9 hours of sleep every night. How much sleep do you enjoy nightly?*

3. What can the group/others do to help you take care of those needs? What kind of support do you need to better meet your needs? What do you need from God to be able to better care for yourself?

4. Why do you think women tend to nurture everyone else, yet ignore their own needs? Is that a biblical way to function?

5. What do you think God is trying to tell you?

Optional Weekly Personal Challenges:

- Make time for a quiet, 30-minute bubble bath. *(physical nurturing)*

- Do a crossword puzzle. *(mental nurturing)*

- Have coffee with a good friend. *(emotional nurturing)*

- Watch an episode of your favorite religious program. *(spiritual nurturing)*

Closing Prayer *(5 minutes)*:

NOTE: Before closing in prayer, take a moment to share personal prayer requests together as a group. Pray for each other throughout the week lifting those needs and requests up to God.

Personal Group Prayer Requests:_____

_____

_____

_____

_____

_____

Father, we know You know our needs even before we do and can trust You to take care of us even when we do not take care of ourselves. Be with us all this week as You help us to identify areas in our lives that need more attention and show us how to fix where we are going astray from Your divine will for our lives. In Jesus' name we pray, Amen.

"You have to create little pockets of joy in your life to take care of yourself."
-Jonathan Van Ness, Entertainer

Notes

_____

_____

_____

_____

_____

_____

_____

_____

_____

_____

_____

_____

_____

_____

_____

_____

_____

_____

_____

_____

WEEK 2: AN ORGANIZED LIFE

Opening Prayer *(5 minutes)*: Lord, we thank You for this time together to grow deeper in our walk with You and our fellowship with each other. We humbly ask You to open our hearts and minds as we receive Your word that it may yield fruit in our lives, deepen our knowledge of You and strengthen our family bonds as children in Your eternal kingdom. May we receive Your favor and blessing upon us as we strive to love more deeply, live godlier lives and become more like You with each passing day. In Jesus' name we pray, Amen.

Ice Breaker *(10 minutes)*: Write down the first and last name of the person sitting to your right. Using only the letters provided in the name, see how many words of at least 3 letters or longer you can make in 60 seconds. All words formed must appear in the Bible somewhere. Who was able to reorganize the letters into the greatest number of words? Who came up with the longest word?

Name:_____

Lesson *(10 minutes)*:

God's Promise: God wants you to have an organized and manageable life.

𝒲eekly 𝒲ord 𝒮tudy

[33] For God is not the author of **confusion**... *1 Corinthians 14:33*

AKATASTASIA (pronounced ak-at-as-tah-see'-ah): This Greek word refers to the instability of a matter. God's preference for how situations unfold is based on order without surrounding chaos to confuse matters. When something has the hallmarks of being in a disorderly state engulfed in randomness that generates confusion, you can be sure that it is not of God. The more order we invite into our lives, the closer we are to living the way God intends us to live.

Scripture Reading:

GOD DESIRES ORDER

[33] For God is not the author of confusion but of peace, as in all the churches of the saints. *1 Corinthians 14:33*

[40] Let all things be done decently and in order. *1 Corinthians 14:40*

[17] Therefore do not be unwise, but understand what the will of the Lord is. *Ephesians 5:17*

GOD CREATED ORDER

[1] To everything there is a season, a time for every purpose under heaven... *Ecclesiastes 3:1*

GOD MAKES ORDER OUT OF DISORDER

[1] In the beginning God created the heavens and the earth. [2] The earth was without form, and void; and darkness was on the face of the deep. And the Spirit of God was hovering over the face of the waters. [3] Then God said, "Let there be light"; and there was light.

[4] And God saw the light, that it was good; and God divided the light from the darkness. [5] God called the light Day, and the darkness He called Night. So, the evening and the morning were the first day. *Genesis 1:1-5*

GOD ASKS US TO EVALUATE OUR OWN LIVES

[3] And why do you look at the speck in your brother's eye, but do not consider the plank in your own eye? *Matthew 7:3*

[11] Now no chastening seems to be joyful for the present, but painful; nevertheless, afterward it yields the peaceable fruit of righteousness to those who have been trained by it. *Hebrews 12:11*

[17] Therefore, to him who knows to do good and does not do it, to him it is sin. *James 4:17*

[20] Now if I do what I will not to do, it is no longer I who do it, but sin that dwells in me. *Romans 7:20*

PLAN AHEAD

[6] Go to the ant, you sluggard! Consider her ways and be wise, [7] which, having no captain, overseer or ruler, [8] provides her supplies in the summer, and gathers her food in the harvest. *Proverbs 6:6-8*

ORGANIZATION TAKES ACTION, NOT PROCRASTINATION

[4] He who observes the wind will not sow, and he who regards the clouds will not reap. *Ecclesiastes 11:4*

[4] He who has a slack hand becomes poor, but the hand of the diligent makes rich. *Proverbs 10:4*

[4] Give no sleep to your eyes, nor slumber to your eyelids. *Proverbs 6:4*

GIVE IT YOUR BEST SHOT

[10] Whatever your hand finds to do, do it with your might...

Ecclesiastes 9:10

KEEP TRYING

[9] And let us not grow weary while doing good, for in due season we shall reap if we do not lose heart. *Galatians 6:9*

EFFORT IS REWARDED WITH SUCCESS

[24] The hand of the diligent will rule, but the lazy man will be put to forced labor. *Proverbs 12:24*

Commentary: Life can be overwhelmingly chaotic at times. Demands from husbands, children, parents, friends and co-workers can have us spinning in every which direction but the one we should be heading. However, chaos is the enemy of all things godly. When life becomes chaotic, order gives way to disorganization and the downward spiral  continues. Even things which are normally manageable appear to become insurmountable obstacles which only threaten to add more fuel to the fire of chaos and confusion. While this type of existence might be Satan's dream for your life, it is not how God intends for us to live.

God invented organization. He gave order to the heavens, the earth and the day and the night at creation. He ordered the seasons to have their appointed times and separated the light from the darkness. And He wants you to have an organized life too. An organized life frees you not just on a physical level, but on mental, emotional and spiritual levels as well. Too often, it is easier to focus on the distractions of daily life or someone else's problems than face what needs to be done in our own lives. When you shift the focus inward and do both inward and outward spring cleaning, the rewards are well worth it.

Evaluate your life and search for areas that could use improvement in the area of organization. When you identify such an area, formulate a plan for what it would require to bring order to the chaos and confusion. Sin creates spiritual clutter in your life and generates emotional turmoil. Many times, by removing unrepentant sin, situations resolve and return to a state of order on many levels. Mentally, a daily "to do" list may help you stay focused and on track during the day. Pursuing order can require bringing something into your life or may demand removing something from your life. For example, adding bins to a certain space may be the solution your situation requires or you may just need to rid excess possessions from your environment to declutter. Financial chaos can be improved by turning your trash into cash. The possibilities are endless. Once you have a plan in place, step into action and make the necessary changes. Do your best and do not be discouraged if your plan takes longer than anticipated or is more arduous than you expected. Attaining true organization can be a long process, but if you stay the course, the rewards will be well worth your time and trouble. Engaging in an organized life is not just an amusing suggestion, but wise advice. So, make the commitment today to declutter your life on every level!

Discussion Questions *(30 minutes)*:

1. On a scale of 1-10, how organized is your life? Why do you think God values order? How does organization affect your relationship with God?

2. Explore the concept of organization from physical, mental, emotional and spiritual perspectives.

3. How do you feel when you walk into a sparsely decorated

room?   A cluttered room?   Do you find order in nature when you are on a walk?

4. What emotional/mental/spiritual baggage are you carrying right now? How can you organize your thoughts?

5. What excuses/distractions do you use to avoid making positive changes in your life?   Do you only make those excuses to yourself of do you make them to God as well?

Optional Weekly Personal Challenges:

- Rearrange books on a shelf grouping them together by size and category. Be sure to locate your Bible where you can easily reach it.

- Hang all the shirts in your closet facing the same direction by type and/or color.

- Group like cans together in the pantry and turn them so all the labels face forward in neat rows.

Organized Living Tips

Writer Morgan Greenwald in an article for *Best Life* website provides the following tips to better organize your life:

- Avoid procrastination.   When you are finished with something, put it away immediately.

- Control impulse shopping.   Only purchase items you are certain that you need.

- Write down your weekly cleaning "to do" items and check them off as you accomplish them.

- Put a Lazy Susan in your refrigerator to manage small food items and condiment bottles.

- Buy a label maker and use it.

Closing Prayer *(5 minutes)*:

NOTE: Before closing in prayer, take a moment to share personal prayer requests together as a group. Pray for each other throughout the week lifting those needs and requests up to God.

Personal Group Prayer Requests:_____

_____

_____

_____

_____

_____

Father, we know You only want the best for each and every one of us. Be with us all this week as You guide us in finding creative ways to organize our lives in every way and on every level. Use our newfound organization as a way to bring us closer to You. In Jesus' name we pray, Amen.

"Divine organization is inherent in all things."
-Marianne Williamson, Author

Notes

_____

_____

_____

_____

_____

_____

_____

_____

_____

_____

_____

_____

_____

_____

_____

_____

_____

_____

WEEK 3: PEOPLE PLEASERS

Opening Prayer *(5 minutes)*: Lord, we thank You for this time together to grow deeper in our walk with You and our fellowship with each other. We humbly ask You to open our hearts and minds as we receive Your word that it may yield fruit in our lives, deepen our knowledge of You and strengthen our family bonds as children in Your eternal kingdom. May we receive Your favor and blessing upon us as we strive to love more deeply, live godlier lives and become more like You with each passing day. In Jesus' name we pray, Amen.

Ice Breaker *(10 minutes)*: Write three positive adjectives that describe the person sitting to your right. Share them with the group along with an explanation about why you chose them.

1. _____

2. _____

3. _____

Lesson *(10 minutes)*:

God's Promise: God will always give us the strength to do the right thing and say the right thing when the time is right.

Ohio State University conducted a study that suggests giving children excessive and unwarranted praise turns them into narcissists.

$\mathcal{W}$eekly $\mathcal{W}$ord $\mathcal{S}$tudy

...[4] and they will turn their ears away from the truth, and be turned aside to **fables**. *2 Timothy 4:4*

MUTHOS (pronounced moo'-thos): When 2 Timothy speaks of fables, the Greek word "muthos" refers to a fictious narrative or story that has been invented as a falsehood. At times, all stories can possess elements of truth, but that does not make the narrative entirely true. Anything that lacks the whole truth can be quite misleading. There are those who will say whatever people want to hear to gain popularity, but that is not a godly approach to relationships or communication. As God's children, we are always to speak the truth in love, even if the other person does not want to receive the truth.

Scripture Reading:

WARN OTHERS

[3] For the time will come when they will not endure sound doctrine, but according to their own desires, because they have itching ears, they will heap up for themselves teachers; [4] and they will turn their ears away from the truth, and be turned aside to fables. *2 Timothy 4:3-4*

[10] For do I now persuade men, or God? Or do I seek to please men? For if I still pleased men, I would not be a bondservant of Christ. *Galatians 1:10*

[17] Son of man, I have made you a watchman for the house of Israel; therefore hear a word from My mouth, and give them warning from Me: [18] When I say to the wicked, "You shall surely die," and you give him no warning, nor speak to warn the wicked from his wicked way, to save his life, that same wicked man shall die in his iniquity; but his blood I will require at your hand. [19] Yet, if you warn the wicked, and he does not turn from his wickedness,

nor from his wicked way, he shall die in his iniquity; but you have delivered your soul. *Ezekiel 3:17-19*

WARN WITH KINDNESS AND TACT

[3] We give no offense in anything, that our ministry may not be blamed. *2 Corinthians 6:3*

[18] But those things which proceed out of the mouth come from the heart, and they defile a man. *Matthew 15:18*

...[15] but, speaking the truth in love... *Ephesians 4:15*

[24] Pleasant words are like a honeycomb, sweetness to the soul and health to the bones. *Proverbs 16:24*

Commentary: Everyone likes to hear good news and pleasant words. But the truth is not always pleasant or fun to hear. God requires us to say something when it is necessary to point something out for another person's well-being. He likens us to watchmen on the wall who bear the responsibility of telling people if we see something not quite right. We are not supposed to keep silent! Our goal should always be to speak the truth even if we know it will not be a popular sentiment or received with gladness. Although people may not always want to hear the truth, God's approval is the only approval we should seek.

However, speaking the truth does not give us the right to be harsh with anyone. We should never say anything with malice in our hearts and our speech should always glorify God. While staying grounded in God's truths, we need to be careful to express ourselves in positive phrases whenever possible. It is the difference between saying, "You're fat!" versus "I think you would be healthier if you lost some weight." The balance between truth and tact is a delicate one, but an important one nonetheless.

Discussion Questions *(30 minutes)*:

1. Are there any truths in your life you do not want to hear?

Is God whispering something to you that you have been turning away from?

2. How do you tell someone a truth they do not want to hear? Is there a way to make the truth more palatable to them? What does it mean to "speak the truth in love" (*Ephesians 4:15*)?

3. Are there times you might be able to phrase something a little more gently? Give an example. When do you find it hard to speak without giving offense (*2 Corinthians 2:6:3*)?

4. How do you try to obtain God's approval? What are some things you can warn other about?

5. Why do you think man's approval matters to people? How does that importance affect your relationship with God?

Optional Weekly Personal Challenges:

- Increase your scripture knowledge by learning one new verse a day for the next week.

- Give someone a genuine compliment every day.

- Tell someone something you have been putting off.

- Say "I love you" more often, especially to God!

Closing Prayer *(5 minutes)*:

NOTE: Before closing in prayer, take a moment to share personal prayer requests together as a group. Pray for each other throughout the week lifting those needs and requests up to God.

Personal Group Prayer Requests:_____

_____

_____

_____

_____

_____

Father, we thank You for giving us the truth and using us as beacons of light in a dark world. Be with us all this week as You teach us through the prompting of the Holy Spirit how to relate to others in Your perfect balance of truth and love. In Jesus' name we pray, Amen.

_____

"You can fool all the people some of the time, and some of the people all the time, but you cannot fool all the people all the time."
-Abraham Lincoln, American President

#

WEEK 4: ALWAYS BE PREPARED

Opening Prayer *(5 minutes)*: Lord, we thank You for this time together to grow deeper in our walk with You and our fellowship with each other. We humbly ask You to open our hearts and minds as we receive Your word that it may yield fruit in our lives, deepen our knowledge of You and strengthen our family bonds as children in Your eternal kingdom. May we receive Your favor and blessing upon us as we strive to love more deeply, live godlier lives and become more like You with each passing day. In Jesus' name we pray, Amen.

Ice Breaker *(10 minutes)*: Using the space provided below, draw a picture of something that happened to you in the past. After everyone has sketched a brief picture, pass your picture to the person sitting to your right. Go around the circle in turn describing what you think the picture represents. Then, have the person who drew the picture describe what actually happened. Keep it fun!

Lesson *(10 minutes)*:

God's Promise: When we do our part, God will do His.

---

*W*eekly *W*ord *S*tudy

...²⁰ faith without **works** is dead. *James 2:20*

ERGON (pronounced er'-gon): In Greek, the word "ergon" means to actively undertake a task. As Christians, our collective task is to proactively go about God's business as we are instructed through His word and the Holy Spirit dwelling within us. Once we choose to have faith in God, that faith must be evident in the choices we make and the steps we take as we go through our daily lives. True faith can always be observed by watching a person's acts and deeds.

Scripture Reading:

GOD PROVIDES

³¹ Therefore do not worry, saying, "What shall we eat?" or "What shall we drink?" or "What shall we wear?" ³² For after all these things the Gentiles seek. For your heavenly Father knows that you need all these things. ³³ But seek first the kingdom of God and His righteousness, and all these things shall be added to you. *Matthew 6:31-33*

¹⁰ Fear not, for I am with you; be not dismayed, for I am your God. I will strengthen you, yes, I will help you, I will uphold you with My righteous right hand. *Isaiah 41:10*

²⁷ Peace I leave with you, My peace I give to you; not as the world gives do I give to you. Let not your heart be troubled, neither let it be afraid. *John 14:27*

²³ Now the king was exceedingly glad for him, and commanded

that they should take Daniel up out of the den. So, Daniel was taken up out of the den, and no injury whatever was found on him, because he believed in his God. *Daniel 6:23*

MAN'S RESPONSIBILITIES

...[20] faith without works is dead. *James 2:20*

[6] Be anxious for nothing, but in everything by prayer and supplication, with thanksgiving, let your requests be made known to God... *Philippians 4:6*

[6] Go to the ant, you sluggard! Consider her ways and be wise, [7] which, having no captain, overseer or ruler, [8] provides her supplies in the summer, and gathers her food in the harvest. [9] How long will you slumber, O sluggard? When will you rise from your sleep? [10] A little sleep, a little slumber, a little folding of the hands to sleep—[11] so shall your poverty come on you like a prowler, and your need like an armed man. *Proverbs 6:6-11*

[12] A prudent man foresees evil and hides himself; the simple pass on and are punished (with consequences). *Proverbs 27:12*

[16] Every prudent man acts with knowledge, but a fool lays open his folly. *Proverbs 13:16*

[6] I planted, Apollos watered, but God gave the increase. *1 Corinthians 3:6*

BIBLICAL DISASTERS

[12] And the rain was on the earth forty days and forty nights. *Genesis 7:12 (Noah's Disaster)*

[54] and the seven years of famine began to come, as Joseph had said. The famine was in all lands, but in all the land of Egypt there was bread. *Genesis 41:54 (Joseph's Disaster)*

[17] So it came to pass, when they (the angels) had brought them

outside, that he said, "Escape for your life! Do not look behind you nor stay anywhere in the plain. Escape to the mountains, lest you be destroyed." *Genesis 19:17 (Lot's Disaster)*

TERMINAL GENERATION

[32] "Now learn this parable from the fig tree: When its branch has already become tender and puts forth leaves, you know that summer is near. [33] So you also, when you see all these things, know that it is near—at the doors! [34] Assuredly, I say to you, this generation will by no means pass away till all these things take place. Matthew 24:32-34

[10] I found Israel like grapes in the wilderness; I saw your fathers as the first fruits on the fig tree in its first season. *Hosea 9:10*

Commentary: There are so many threats that can lead to potential disasters in our turbulent world today—economic collapse, rising food prices, bioterrorism, wars, pandemics, solar threats, hurricanes, earthquakes, super volcano's, EMP's, cyber attacks, etc. that it is impossible to prepare for everything. Life has the uncanny ability to turn on a dime in completely unforeseen ways at the most inopportune time. But we do not have to worry or be afraid. God will guide each one of us in the direction appropriate for the challenges He knows we will each uniquely face. Joseph had to prepare for a seven-year disaster and God made a way for him to be in a position of power so that he could make the necessary preparations. Noah's disaster lasted forty days and nights. God enabled him to prepare in advance too. Lot, on the other hand, had to flee on a moment's notice. Even then, God still enabled his needs to be met that he might live.

Having faith that God will provide for our every need does not relieve us of our obligation to do what we can when we can. After we have prayerfully sought God's guidance, God expects us to use the brain and resources He gave us to take appropriate actions whenever it would be prudent to do so. It may be God who makes the seeds of a garden grow, but He still expects man to plant and water the garden.

Discussion Questions *(30 minutes)*:

1. How prepared do you think you are for an unexpected disaster? What type of events worry you? How do you think Noah, Joseph and Lot felt about their disasters respectively?

2. If a disaster were to occur, how long could you go before you would need some form of help or assistance either divine or otherwise? What do you think would be a good goal to have for an amount of time you should be prepared to "go it alone" (i.e. be prepared for 72 hours, 2 weeks, a month, 6 months, a year, 3 years, longer)?

3. What type of preparations do you think Noah (40 days), Joseph (7 years) and Lot (fled instantly) did to prepare for their respective disasters? What type of divine assistance do you think Noah, Joseph and Lot received for their survival?

4. What steps do you think God wants you to take right now, where you are at, to become more prepared for unforeseen events?

According to the Provident Living Food Storage Calculator, a family of four (two adults with two children under twelve) should have a 52-week supply of food on hand including:

Grain	1320 lbs.
Legumes	198 lbs.
Dairy Products	99 lbs.
Sugars	198 lbs.
Leavening Agents	20 lbs.
Salt	20 lbs.
Fats	99 lbs.

5. In order of importance, how would you rate the following: food, shelter, money, clothes, comforts, protection/self-defense?

6. Do you believe we are the "Terminal Generation" referred to in the Bible who will see the return of Jesus and that we will see unprecedented events in our lifetime leading up to the Tribulation? If you do believe we are the Terminal Generation, how does that affect your preparations for the future both physically and spiritually?

Optional Weekly Personal Challenges:

- Develop a food security strategy for your family by learning how to can and store food at home for both short-term and long-term needs. Your plan should include starting a garden. If you currently practice gardening, take your skills to the next level or expand your garden.

- Volunteer at church. In doing so, you will form stronger bonds with other Christians creating a support network for yourself and your family if you ever need to tap into it.

- Read *Are We the Terminal Generation?* by Christine Tate.

- Take a CPR course to be able to provide emergency support to someone in need.

Closing Prayer *(5 minutes)*:

NOTE: Before closing in prayer, take a moment to share personal prayer requests together as a group. Pray for each other throughout the week lifting those needs and requests up to God.

Personal Group Prayer Requests:_____

_____

_____

_____

_____

_____

Father, we trust You to take care of us in whatever circumstance we encounter. We acknowledge that You desire for us to do whatever we can whenever we can to help ourselves and others. Show us this week what You would have us do to take whatever steps would be prudent for us to take towards that goal. In Jesus' name we pray, Amen.

_____

"Americans do not have a good track record when it comes to preparing for disasters, unless they see a clear possibility of personally being in harms way."

-Irwin Redlener, Activist

Notes

WEEK 5: WEIGHT MANAGEMENT

Opening Prayer *(5 minutes)*: Lord, we thank You for this time together to grow deeper in our walk with You and our fellowship with each other. We humbly ask You to open our hearts and minds as we receive Your word that it may yield fruit in our lives, deepen our knowledge of You and strengthen our family bonds as children in Your eternal kingdom. May we receive Your favor and blessing upon us as we strive to love more deeply, live godlier lives and become more like You with each passing day. In Jesus' name we pray, Amen.

Ice Breaker *(10 minutes)*: Begin by having everyone test their knowledge of Bible trivia. Set a time limit of 5 minutes. Then, check the answers in the appendix at the back of the book. Score one point for each correct answer given (50 possible points). Who scored the highest?

1. How many of each animal did Noah bring onto the Ark?
    _____

2. What does the Devil look like?
    _____

3. Where is the Devil right now?
    _____

4. Who is the oldest man in the Bible?
    _____

5. How many horses did Solomon have?
    _____

6. In ancient Israel, how did men close deals?
    _____

7. Name all 10 commandments: (score one point for each correct commandment listed and score one additional point for each one listed in the correct placement order—20 points possible).

    1st: _____

    2nd: _____

    3rd: _____

4th: _____

5th: _____

6th: _____

7th: _____

8th: _____

9th: _____

10th: _____

8. What is the shortest chapter in the Bible?_____

9. How old was Adam when he died?_____

10. What type of fruit was the "forbidden fruit" Eve ate from the Tree of Life?_____

11. Do aliens exist?_____

12. How many names did Jesus have? (score one point for each name—15 possible points max):_____

_____

_____

_____

_____

_____

_____

Lesson (10 minutes):

God's Promise: God knows how to get us from point A to point B and will get us there despite our human weaknesses and lack of perspective.

𝒲eekly 𝒲ord 𝒮tudy

...[19] your body is the **temple** of the Holy Spirit who is in you...
1 Corinthians 6:19

NAOS (pronounced nah-os'): More than just referring to the general temple in Jerusalem, the Greek word "naos" specifically points to the sanctuary within the Jerusalem temple consisting of the Holy of Holies. The Holy of Holies was the most sacred part of God's house. Linking the holiest part of the Jerusalem temple with our mortal body suggests that we are to care for our bodies in the same intentional, careful and reverent manner that the Jewish people cared for God's innermost sanctuary. Being mindful of our health and the negative consequences of unhealthy patterns is one way we can honor God's temple in our bodies. Our bodies truly are God's sanctuary.

Scripture Reading:

THE NECESSITY OF GOD

...[5] for without Me you can do nothing. *John 15:5*

BE HEALTHY

[19] Or do you not know that your body is the temple of the Holy Spirit who is in you, whom you have from God, and you are not your own? *1 Corinthians 6:19*

[2] Beloved, I pray that you may prosper in all things and be in health, just as your soul prospers. [3] For I rejoiced greatly when brethren came and testified of the truth that is in you, just as you walk in the truth. [4] I have no greater joy than to hear that my children walk in truth. *3 John 1:2-4*

FOCUS ON TODAY

[34] Therefore do not worry about tomorrow, for tomorrow will worry about its own things. Sufficient for the day is its own trouble. *Matthew 6:34*

ACTIONS

[5] Let your moderation be known unto all men. *Philippians 4:5 (KJV)*

[2] And put a knife to your throat if you are a man given to appetite. *Proverbs 23:2*

[16] Have you found honey? Eat only as much as you need, lest you be filled with it and vomit. *Proverbs 25:16*

Commentary: The first step to weight management is simply honestly admitting you need to do something. Like the quiz in today's Ice Breaker, sometimes we think we know things and are seeing things correctly, but if we look deeper, we realize a degree of ignorance somewhere. We all need to brush the curtain back and see things for how they indeed are, not what we wish they would be. No more excuses. Call a spade a spade. Face reality as it is, not what you wish reality was or hope reality will be.

Health and weight are intimately connected. God loves us and wants us to be healthy which includes maintaining a healthy weight. After we face reality, we need to commit to the process. Since only God knows everything, only He can get us across the finish line of weight loss. He knows what we need to do to successfully lose weight even when we do not. But He does give us some specific advice to follow: eat in moderation, limit sweets, control your appetite and take things one day at a time. You cannot do anything about yesterday and tomorrow is not here yet. Today is what matters. When you spend time and energy worrying about yesterday or planning for tomorrow, you rob yourself of the profitability of what you can do today. Take things one baby step at a time. And above all, remember to pray!

OAT MILK

The *Farmer's Almanac* touts the benefits of oat milk. Oat milk with no added sugars is dairy-free and a wonderful milk substitute for people who are lactose intolerant, gluten sensitive or prone to allergies. Even for those who can tolerate dairy well, oat milk is reportedly beneficial in lowering cholesterol and controlling blood glucose levels. Boasting a thicker, creamier consistency, oat milk is also a favorite substitute for milk in coffee or tea due to its resistance to curdling when added to hot beverages. To make your own homemade oat milk, follow these easy steps:

1. Add two parts water to one part dry, uncooked, old-fashioned oats or oat groats.
2. Cover oats to rest overnight.
3. The next morning, strain oats through a fine sieve or cheesecloth separating the liquid from the oats.

With a variety of uses, oat milk can be:

- Poured over cereal
- Added to coffee or tea
- Used to thicken gravies and sauces
- A base for making a smoothie or chocolate milk (add cocoa powder, a few drops of vanilla and a little sweetener)
- Substitute for milk when baking
- Oat milk can even be used to make yogurt, kefir and ice-cream

Discussion Questions *(30 minutes)*:

1. Have you faced the truth about your weight or do you have blinders on? What is the body image you hold of yourself in your mind?

2. How do you think your body image affects your self-esteem and ability to believe God loves you?

3. What steps are you willing to take right now to lose weight and/or be healthier? What do you think God wants you to do to be healthier?

4. How much food do you really need in a day? How do you personally define "moderation"? How does God define "moderation"?

5. Do you pay attention to the quality of the food you put in your body? Does God approve of food grown with pesticides, processed food with added chemicals or food grown from genetically modified seeds?

6. How would you rate your body in terms of being the temple within which the Holy Spirit resides (*1 Corinthians 6:19*)?

Optional Weekly Personal Challenges:

- Make small changes wherever you can.

- Make one healthy food substitution this week (i.e. cottage cheese blended with lemon juice in place of sour cream)

- Take the stairs instead of the elevator this week whenever you can.

- Do a few minor stretches before getting out of bed in the morning.

Closing Prayer *(5 minutes)*:

NOTE: Before closing in prayer, take a moment to share personal prayer requests together as a group. Pray for each other *throughout the week lifting those needs and requests up to God.*

Personal Group Prayer Requests:_____

_____

_____

_____

_____

_____

Father, we admit we can do nothing apart from You. Guide us and strengthen us as we make small changes this week to be healthier mothers, wives, daughters, friends and neighbors. In Jesus' name we pray, Amen.

"When your body absorbs toxins, it stores them in fat, which is why fiber and probiotics are strategic weapons for weight loss. Fiber keeps your colon healthy and reduces your body's absorption of toxins."
-Suzanne Somers, Actress and Author

Notes

_____

_____

_____

_____

_____

_____

_____

_____

_____

_____

_____

_____

_____

_____

_____

_____

_____

_____

_____

_____

_____

_____

_____

WEEK 6: CHRISTIAN RELATIONSHIPS

Opening Prayer *(5 minutes)*: Lord, we thank You for this time together to grow deeper in our walk with You and our fellowship with each other. We humbly ask You to open our hearts and minds as we receive Your word that it may yield fruit in our lives, deepen our knowledge of You and strengthen our family bonds as children in Your eternal kingdom. May we receive Your favor and blessing upon us as we strive to love more deeply, live godlier lives and become more like You with each passing day. In Jesus' name we pray, Amen.

Ice Breaker *(10 minutes)*: Have every other person turn toward the person sitting to their right so everyone has a partner. If the group has an odd number, have one team of three. Each team must come up with one thing they each have in common. It cannot be anything obvious like all living in the same city, all attending the same Bible study, etc. When each team has identified one commonality each person in the group shares, join each team with another team and have the new group of four repeat the process to find the one thing all four of them have in common. Then have the groups of four pair with another group of four to make a group of eight and repeat the process until everyone is one group again and the group has identified the one thing everyone has in common.

Lesson *(10 minutes)*:

God's Promise: We are all connected through God and by treating people the way God instructs you to treat people, your life will be filled with happy, healthy and fulfilling relationships.

𝒲eekly 𝒲ord 𝒮tudy

[33] But seek **first** the kingdom of God... *Matthew 6:33*

PROTON (pronounced pro'-ton): To put something first as in the Greek word "proton" means to prioritize that thing above all else in time, place, rank, influence and honor. We were made by our Creator to be in relationship with others, but those relationships should never come before God in any way. Spend as much time with God as you do with your earthly loved ones. Give God a place of honor in your life and make Him the center of all of your other relationships. Let God's influence in your life be evident in how you interact with others and you will be blessed in those relationships for it.

Scripture Reading:

GOD COMES FIRST

[33] But seek first the kingdom of God and His righteousness, and all these things shall be added to you. *Matthew 6:33*

[30] And you shall love the LORD your God with all your heart, with all your soul, with all your mind, and with all your strength. This is the first commandment. *Mark 12:30*

[37] He who loves father or mother more than Me is not worthy of Me. And he who loves son or daughter more than Me is not worthy of Me. *Matthew 10:37*

FELLOWSHIP WITH OTHERS

[18] And the LORD God said, "It is not good that man should be alone; I will make him a helper comparable to him." *Genesis 2:18*

[14] Do not be unequally yoked together with unbelievers. For what fellowship has righteousness with lawlessness? And what

communion has light with darkness? *2 Corinthians 6:14*

3 Can two walk together, unless they are agreed? *Amos 3:3*

2 Let each of us please his neighbor for his good, leading to edification. *Romans 15:2*

9 You shall love your neighbor as yourself. *Romans 13:9*

19 So then, my beloved brethren, let every man be swift to hear, slow to speak, slow to wrath... *James 1:19*

6 Let your speech always be with grace, seasoned with salt, that you may know how you ought to answer each one. *Colossians 4:6*

...2 with all lowliness and gentleness, with longsuffering, bearing with one another in love, 3 endeavoring to keep the unity of the Spirit in the bond of peace. *Ephesians 4:2-3*

4 Love suffers long and is kind; love does not envy; love does not parade itself, is not puffed up; 5 does not behave rudely, does not seek its own, is not provoked, thinks no evil; 6 does not rejoice in iniquity, but rejoices in the truth; 7 bears all things, believes all things, hopes all things, endures all things. 8 Love never fails. But whether there are prophecies, they will fail; whether there are tongues, they will cease; whether there is knowledge, it will vanish away. *1 Corinthians 13:4-8*

24 And let us consider one another in order to stir up love and good works, 25 not forsaking the assembling of ourselves together, as is the manner of some, but exhorting one another, and so much the more as you see the Day approaching. *Hebrews 10:24-25*

Commentary: It was never God's will for humans to be alone. God wants us to have happy, healthy, rewarding relationships in our lives. The Bible is life's little instruction book and it gives us clear guidelines on just how to make that happen. To get there,

God makes it clear we must put our relationship with Him first before all other relationships. Spend time getting to know God by reading the Bible and praying often. If you had a friend you rarely spoke to, how strong do you think that relationship would be? The same principle applies to having a relationship with God. He wants to know us and love us, but we have to want to know and love Him back.

Once your focus is clearly on God, it is important to make sure all your close and important relationships are Christian relationships. We are to seek strong bonds with other believers. Everyone you draw close to and depend on should be a Christian. That does not mean every Christian relationship you form will be perfect and without trials, but sharing a common set of beliefs and values

---

Relationship Health Checklist

Vanderbilt Health suggests the following behaviors contribute to healthy relationships. In your relationships, do you:

- ☐ Listen to the other person more than you talk about yourself?
- ☐ Communicate in a way the other person can understand?
- ☐ Exhibit a positive attitude and dispense compliments generously?
- ☐ Show your appreciation and demonstrate social graces?
- ☐ Compromise when disagreements arise?
- ☐ Ignore the small stuff and focus on genuine priorities that truly matter?
- ☐ Spend time together sharing in the other person's hobbies and interests?
- ☐ Offer forgiveness freely when necessary?
- ☐ Carry the other person's burdens and provide help whenever and wherever you find the opportunity?
- ☐ Have realistic in your expectations?

---

centered around a strong shared faith creates an enduring foundation for the relationship to thrive.

Relationships require godly maintenance. Nurture them with mutual love and encouragement, always being mindful of how our speech can affect others. Careless words spoken can cause irreparable damage. Learn how to relate to others as God would have you relate by His standards. If we follow His rules for our life and relationships, we can look forward to many rewarding and fulfilling experiences.

Discussion Questions *(30 minutes)*:

1. What do you need to do in your life to build a stronger relationship with God?

2. Identify a relationship in your life that could use some improvement. What part(s) of that relationship vary from God's prescription for healthy relationships?

3. What concrete steps can you take to improve that relationship?

4. Are most of your important relationships with other Christians or non-Christians? How does that affect your walk as a Christian?

5. How do you define being a Christian? What does being a Christian mean to you?

Optional Weekly Personal Challenges:

- Increase the amount of time you spend talking to God each day.

- Call a friend or a family member you have not spoken to in a while.

- Thank people, including God, more often.

- Send an "I'm Thinking of You" card to someone.

Closing Prayer *(5 minutes)*:

NOTE: Before closing in prayer, take a moment to share personal prayer requests together as a group. Pray for each other throughout the week lifting those needs and requests up to God.

Personal Group Prayer Requests:_____

_____

_____

_____

_____

_____

Father, thank You for the wonderful relationships You have brought and will bring into our lives. We ask You to heal those relationships in our lives that need healing, strengthen those relationships that need strengthening, rid us of toxic and unhealthy relationships and bring new Christian relationships into our hearts and lives for we know that is Your will for us. In Jesus' name we pray, Amen.

"Earthly wisdom is doing what comes naturally. Godly wisdom is doing what the Holy Spirit compels us to do."

-Charles Stanley, Pastor and Author

Notes

_____

_____

_____

_____

_____

_____

_____

_____

_____

_____

_____

_____

_____

_____

_____

_____

_____

_____

_____

_____

_____

_____

WEEK 7: BEING A VIRTUOUS WOMAN

Opening Prayer *(5 minutes)***:** Lord, we thank You for this time together to grow deeper in our walk with You and our fellowship with each other. We humbly ask You to open our hearts and minds as we receive Your word that it may yield fruit in our lives, deepen our knowledge of You and strengthen our family bonds as children in Your eternal kingdom. May we receive Your favor and blessing upon us as we strive to love more deeply, live godlier lives and become more like You with each passing day. In Jesus' name we pray, Amen.

Ice Breaker *(10 minutes)***:** Using the list on this and the next page, allow 5 minutes for each group member to match all group members with a Bible character. Then, go around the room and share which Bible character each group member picked for each person and why. You do not need to choose a character for yourself.

ABIGAIL: Nabal's wife who became David's wife after Nabal (wicked man) died.

ANNA: Older Jewish prophetess who prophesied about Jesus.

BATHSHEBA: Uriah the Hittite's wife. After Uriah died, married David and became Solomon's mother.

DEBORAH: Prophetess and the only female judge in the Old Testament.

DELILAH: The woman Sampson loved who ultimately led to his destruction.

ESTHER: Queen and wife of Ahasuerus.

EVE: Adam's wife and first woman.

HAGAR: Abraham's concubine and handmaiden of Sarah. Later became Ishmael's mother.

JOANNA: One of the women who prepared Jesus' body for burial.

LEAH: Jacob's first wife who he was tricked into marrying instead of Rachel, the real woman he loved.

LYDIA: One of the first women to convert to Christianity.

MARY: Jesus' mother.

MARY MAGDALENE: Jesus' disciple.

MIRIAM: Moses' sister.

NAOMI: Mother-in-law to Ruth.

PHAROAH'S DAUGHTER: Moses' adopted mother.

RACHEL: Jacob's second wife and Leah's sister.

RUTH: Obed's wife and key figure in the lineage of Jesus.

SARAH: Abraham's wife and mother of Isaac.

ZIPPORAH: Moses' wife.

OTHER: List your own favorite woman in the Bible.

GROUP MEMBER   BIBLE CHARACTER

_____	_____
_____	_____
_____	_____
_____	_____
_____	_____
_____	_____
_____	_____

Lesson *(10 minutes)*:

God's Promise: When your actions are a glory to God, your efforts will not be in vain.

Weekly Word Study

[10] Who can find a **virtuous** wife? *Proverbs 31:10-31*

CHAYIL (pronounced khah'-yil): When a woman is defined by the Hebrew word "Chayil", she is strong and competent with many abilities. A force to be reckoned with in her own right, a wife who is virtuous can independently take care of herself and the rest of her household as well. Efficient in all that she does, she is a woman of substance who is a wealth of many valuable resources and knows how to use the resources at her disposal.

Scripture Reading:

GOD'S DESCRIPTION OF A VIRTUOUS WOMAN

[10] Who can find a virtuous wife? For her worth is far above rubies.

[11] The heart of her husband safely trusts her; so, he will have no lack of gain.

[12] She does him good and not evil all the days of her life.

[13] She seeks wool and flax, and willingly works with her hands.

[14] She is like the merchant ships; she brings her food from afar.

[15] She also rises while it is yet night, and provides food for her household, and a portion for her maidservants.

¹⁶ She considers a field and buys it; from her profits she plants a vineyard.

¹⁷ She girds herself with strength, and strengthens her arms.

¹⁸ She perceives that her merchandise is good, and her lamp does not go out by night.

¹⁹ She stretches out her hands to the distaff, and her hand holds the spindle.

²⁰ She extends her hand to the poor, yes, she reaches out her hands to the needy.

²¹ She is not afraid of snow for her household, for all her household is clothed with scarlet.

²² She makes tapestry for herself; her clothing is fine linen and purple.

²³ Her husband is known in the gates, when he sits among the elders of the land.

²⁴ She makes linen garments and sells them, and supplies sashes for the merchants.

²⁵ Strength and honor are her clothing; she shall rejoice in time to come.

²⁶ She opens her mouth with wisdom, and on her tongue is the law of kindness.

²⁷ She watches over the ways of her household, and does not eat the bread of idleness.

²⁸ Her children rise up and call her blessed; her husband also, and he praises her: ²⁹ "Many daughters have done well, but you excel

them all."

[30] Charm is deceitful and beauty is passing, but a woman who fears the LORD, she shall be praised.

[31] Give her of the fruit of her hands, and let her own works praise her in the gates. *Proverbs 31:10-31*

Commentary: We all want to put our best foot forward, but for the Christian woman, that also means being a virtuous woman. *Collin's Dictionary* defines "virtue" as:

> VIRTUE: 1. Right action and thinking. 2. A specific moral quality regarded as good or meritorious.

"Right action and right thinking" for a Christian encompasses meditating on God's law, discerning His will for your life and then acting upon that information in tangible ways. For the woman in this proverb, her right actions entail acquiring necessary goods for the running of her household (v. 13 and 14), feeding those in her household (v. 15), managing a staff of servants and overseeing household affairs (v. 15 and 27), rising early and staying up late to maximize her productivity (v. 15 and 18), being financially savvy and developing both real estate and retail businesses (v. 16 and 24), growing her own food (v. 16), exercising (v. 17), participating in charity work (v. 20), and engaging in creative pursuits (v. 22).

Aside from "right actions", a virtuous woman must have "right thinking". "Right thinking" produces fruit of the spirit that is evident to the rest of the world. For the virtuous woman in this proverb, "right thinking" led to a right heart. Having a right heart led her husband to trust her (v. 11), cultivated a fearless attitude within her (v. 21), drove others to perceive her as strong and esteem her in high regard (v. 25), allowed her to speak with wisdom (v. 26), and caused both her husband and her children to sing her praises (v. 28).

Virtuous women cultivate intangible qualities such as

trustworthiness (v. 11) and industriousness (v. 13). In addition to being held in high regard by others, the rewards of being a virtuous woman include being fruitful (v. 11) and receiving recognition (v. 23). More than just looking her best, the virtuous woman's deeds speak for themselves. And they get her noticed. If we do the right things and please God, we can be assured that all else will fall into place.

Discussion Questions *(30 minutes)*:

1. What does the word "virtue" mean to you? How does the dictionary's definition of "virtue" as presented in the commentary compare or contrast to the Hebrew definition

```
INDEPENDENT AND PART-TIME BUSINESS IDEAS

Blogging/Writing
In-Home Childcare
Etsy/Shopify Craft Store
Virtual Assistant
Rent-a-Wife/Errand Service
Maid Service
Catering Services
Baking Cookies, Cakes, etc.
Meal Services (Personal Chef)
Online Teaching
Website Design
Photography
Gardening/Landscaping Services
Growing specialty food items
     for local restaurants
Wedding Planning
Fitness Class Instructor
Personal Trainer
Soap or Candle Making
Companion/Caregiver for
     Senior Citizens
Uber Driver
```

of "virtuous" given in the word study section?

2. What actions in your life would cause someone to refer to you as "virtuous"? Is that an accurate reflection of God's portrait of the Virtuous Woman?

3. Who are the women/role models in your life that you would call virtuous? Why? What makes them virtuous?

4. How can you be a good role model and demonstrate godly virtue to other women and young girls?

5. Verse 27 states that a virtuous woman does not "eat the bread of idleness". How much of your life is spent in idleness? What new skills/abilities would you like to learn/expand/develop to become a more virtuous woman?

Optional Weekly Personal Challenges:

- Start a small side business you can develop in your spare time. Donate the profits to your church or a local charity.

- Donate a bag of food to a soup kitchen.

- Bake a loaf of bread from scratch.

- Learn a new skill (knitting, crocheting, sewing, take a college class, martial arts, etc.)

Closing Prayer *(5 minutes)*:

NOTE: Before closing in prayer, take a moment to share personal prayer requests together as a group. Pray for each other throughout the week lifting those needs and requests up to God.

Personal Group Prayer Requests:_____

_____

_____

_____

_____

_____

Father, we recognize that You are the source of all virtue. Let all of our actions be a glory to You that all may see Your light shining through us as the light of the world. Be with us all this week as You show us ways we can be more virtuous every day in every way. In Jesus' name we pray, Amen.

"The happiness of your life depends upon the quality of your thought: therefore, guard accordingly, and take care that you entertain no notions unsuitable to virtue and reasonable nature."

-Marcus Aurelius, Roman Leader

Notes

_____

_____

_____

_____

_____

_____

_____

_____

_____

_____

_____

_____

_____

_____

_____

_____

_____

_____

WEEK 8: FINANCIAL HEALTH

Opening Prayer *(5 minutes)*: Lord, we thank You for this time together to grow deeper in our walk with You and our fellowship with each other. We humbly ask You to open our hearts and minds as we receive Your word that it may yield fruit in our lives, deepen our knowledge of You and strengthen our family bonds as children in Your eternal kingdom. May we receive Your favor and blessing upon us as we strive to love more deeply, live godlier lives and become more like You with each passing day. In Jesus' name we pray, Amen.

Ice Breaker *(10 minutes)*: By now, you have had a chance to get to know your fellow group members on a more personal level. Since it can sometimes be easier to see what someone else needs instead of identifying our own needs, each person will make three short-term, achievable resolutions for the person sitting two places to their left based on what they have learned about the person during the course of this study. The resolutions should be things that the person can begin to work on immediately. When everyone is finished, go around the circle and share the resolutions you chose and why with the rest of the group. Another variation of this activity is for the group as a whole to make three resolutions for each person in the group. The person receiving the resolutions should not offer ideas when it is their turn to receive resolutions. Remember to give suggestions for resolutions with a loving spirit and receive outside insights with a thankful and open heart.

RESOLUTIONS MY GROUP SUGGESTED FOR ME:

1.

2.

3.

Lesson *(10 minutes)*:

God's Promise: God will bless you in many ways for your faithfulness to Him.

---

*W*eekly *W*ord *S*tudy

[8] **Owe** no one anything... *Romans 13:8*

OPHEILO (pronounced of-i'-lo):   In this passage of scripture, the Greek word "opheilo" refers to money. As good stewards of God's financial blessings, it should be our ultimate goal to be completely debt-free. However, "opheilo" can also be used as a metaphor for owing goodwill to someone. In this sense of the word, not only are we to refrain from mingling finances with others, but owing non-financial favors to other people is prohibited as well.

Scripture Reading:

TITHING

[10] "Bring all the tithes into the storehouse, that there may be food in My house, and try Me now in this," says the LORD of hosts, "If I will not open for you the windows of heaven and pour out for you such blessing that there will not be room enough to receive it." *Malachi 3:10*

[6] But this I say: He who sows sparingly will also reap sparingly, and he who sows bountifully will also reap bountifully. [7] So let each one give as he purposes in his heart, not grudgingly or of necessity; for God loves a cheerful giver. [8] And God is able to make all grace abound toward you, that you, always having all sufficiency in all things, may have an abundance for every good work. *2 Corinthians 9:6-8*

DEBT

[7] The rich rules over the poor, and the borrower is servant to the lender. *Proverbs 22:7*

[8] Owe no one anything except to love one another, for he who loves another has fulfilled the law. *Romans 13:8*

SAVING

[2] On the first day of the week let each one of you lay something aside, storing up as he may prosper, that there be no collections when I come. *1 Corinthians 16:2*

SALARY

[14] Likewise the soldiers asked him, saying, "And what shall we do?" So, he said to them, "Do not intimidate anyone or accuse falsely, and be content with your wages." *Luke 3:14*

DIVERSIFICATION

[2] Give (divide) a serving to seven, and also to eight, for you do not know what evil will be on the earth. *Ecclesiastes 11:2*

TAXES

...[21] And He (Jesus) said to them, "Render therefore to Caesar the things that are Caesar's, and to God the things that are God's." *Matthew 22:21*

SOURCE OF CHRISTIAN WEALTH

[18] And you shall remember the LORD your God, for it is He who gives you power to get wealth, that He may establish His covenant which He swore to your fathers, as it is this day. *Deuteronomy 8:18*

[27] John answered and said, "A man can receive nothing unless it has been given to him from heaven." *John 3:27*

[9] The LORD your God will make you abound in all the work of your hand, in the fruit of your body, in the increase of your livestock, and in the produce of your land for good. For the LORD will again rejoice over you for good as He rejoiced over your fathers... *Deuteronomy 30:9*

[25] I have been young, and now am old; yet I have not seen the righteous forsaken, nor his descendants begging bread. *Psalm 37:25*

[22] The blessing of the LORD makes one rich, and He adds no sorrow with it. *Proverbs 10:22*

TEMPORAL NATURE OF MATERIAL GOODS

[7] For we brought nothing into this world, and it is certain we can carry nothing out. *1 Timothy 6:7*

Commentary: Like the Ice Breaker activity today, financial health requires forethought and planning. God wants to bless us, but we have to receive that blessing in obedience to Him. When acting in obedience to God's guidance, it should be the goal of every believer to be debt-free. In today's world, getting there can be a challenge. God also wants us to work hard and put aside savings for a rainy day. We are to be content with the money He has given us through our wages and not begrudge paying taxes. But, most importantly, we are to tithe. In God's divine order, we cannot receive unless we first give away. It is the only place in the Bible where we are given direct permission to test God in something. This wisdom is contrary to the wisdom of the world, but we must believe God that this is the path through which He will bless us. Do not be afraid to step out in faith by giving back to God generously that which He has so richly first given us.

Discussion Questions *(30 minutes)*:

1. What role do possessions have in your life? What are your feelings about money? How do you think God views money?

2. How would you feel if you lost everything you owned? Why?

3. Why do you think the world's wisdom is backwards from God's wisdom (i.e. hold on to what you have to gain more vs. give away first to gain increase)?

4. Is the concept of tithing easy or hard for you to accept? Why? Are you a tither?

5. What do you consider "a good investment" in today's economic forum? Would God agree and why?

Optional Weekly Personal Challenges:

- Put a dollar a day in a special cookie jar that you never touch.

- Write your first tithing check out to your church. If you all ready tithe, make a special offering.

Did You Know?

According to a Pew Research Center survey in 2018:
- 19% of American adults are financially considered upper income households.
- 52% of American adults are financially considered middle income households.
- 29% of American adults are financially considered lower income households.

Adjusting for the cost of living in a metropolitan area with a 2016 dollar value, a three person family would need to earn the following amounts to be considered in each category:
- Incomes greater than $135,600 are considered Upper Class.
- Incomes between $45,200 - $135,600 are considered Middle Class .
- Incomes less than $45,200 are considered Lower Class.

- Do one thing that will make you a better employee (or homemaker if you are not employed).

- Make a five-year financial plan and a long-term financial plan. Be sure to verify that you will have earned your social security credits before you retire.

- Give something away or sell something you do not need that has outlived its usefulness in your life on eBay.

Closing Prayer *(5 minutes)*:

NOTE: Before closing in prayer, take a moment to share personal prayer requests together as a group. Pray for each other throughout the week lifting those needs and requests up to God.

Personal Group Prayer Requests:_____

_____

_____

_____

_____

_____

Father, we know that all prosperity and success is a divine gift from You. We ask Your blessing on the financial situation of everyone in this group. Prosper us all that we may be better givers for Your kingdom. In Jesus' name we pray, Amen.

"If you make money your god, it will plague you like the devil."

-Henry Fielding, Novelist

Notes

_____

_____

_____

_____

_____

_____

_____

_____

_____

_____

_____

_____

_____

_____

_____

_____

_____

_____

_____

_____

_____

_____

APPENDIX

ANSWERS TO WEEK 5 QUIZ

1. 2 of each unclean animal and 7 of each clean animal.

> [2] You shall take with you seven each of every clean animal, a male and his female; two each of animals that are unclean, a male and his female; [3] also seven each of birds of the air, male and female, to keep the species alive on the face of all the earth. *Genesis 7:2-3*

2. A beautiful angel of light

> [14] And no wonder! For Satan himself transforms himself into an angel of light. *2 Corinthians 11:14*

3. Roaming the earth looking for people to tempt and destroy

> [8] Be sober, be vigilant; because your adversary the devil walks about like a roaring lion, seeking whom he may devour. *1 Peter 5:8*

4. Methuselah

> [27] So all the days of Methuselah were nine hundred and sixty-nine years; and he died. *Genesis 5:27*

5. 12,000

> [26] Solomon had forty thousand stalls of horses for his chariots, and twelve thousand horsemen. *1 Kings 4:26*

6. Exchanging Sandals

> [7] Now this was the custom in former times in Israel concerning redeeming and exchanging, to confirm anything: one man took off his sandal and gave it to

the other, and this was a confirmation in Israel. *Ruth 4:7*

7. 1st Commandment

> [3] You shall have no other gods before me. *Exodus 20:3*

2nd Commandment

> [4] You shall not make for yourself a carved image— any likeness of anything that is in heaven above, or that is in the earth beneath, or that is in the water under the earth; [5] you shall not bow down to them nor serve them. For I, the LORD your God, am a jealous God, visiting the iniquity of the fathers upon the children to the third and fourth generations of those who hate Me, [6] but showing mercy to thousands, to those who love Me and keep My commandments. *Exodus 20:4-6*

3rd Commandment

> [7] You shall not take the name of the LORD your God in vain, for the LORD will not hold him guiltless who takes His name in vain. *Exodus 20:7*

4th Commandment

> [8] Remember the Sabbath day, to keep it holy. [9] Six days you shall labor and do all your work, [10] but the seventh day is the Sabbath of the LORD your God. In it you shall do no work: you, nor your son, nor your daughter, nor your male servant, nor your female servant, nor your cattle, nor your stranger who is within your gates. [11] For in six days the LORD made the heavens and the earth, the sea, and all that is in them, and rested the seventh day.

Therefore, the LORD blessed the Sabbath day and hallowed it. *Exodus 20:8-11*

5th Commandment

[12] Honor your father and your mother, that your days may be long upon the land which the LORD your God is giving you. *Exodus 20:12*

6th Commandment

[13] You shall not murder. *Exodus 20:13*

7th Commandment

[14] You shall not commit adultery. *Exodus 20:14*

8th Commandment

[15] You shall not steal. *Exodus 20:15*

9th Commandment

[16] You shall not bear false witness against your neighbor. *Exodus 20:16*

10th Commandment

[17] You shall not covet your neighbor's house; you shall not covet your neighbor's wife, nor his male servant, nor his female servant, nor his ox, nor his donkey, nor anything that is your neighbor's. *Exodus 20:17*

8. Psalm 117 has only 2 verses.

[1] Praise the LORD, all you Gentiles! Laud Him, all you peoples! [2] For His merciful kindness is great

toward us, and the truth of the LORD endures forever. Praise the LORD! *Psalm 117:1-2*

9. 930

5 So all the days that Adam lived were nine hundred and thirty years; and he died. *Genesis 5:5*

10. The Bible never identifies the specific type of fruit Eve eats and offers to Adam.

6 So when the woman saw that the tree was good for food, that it was pleasant to the eyes, and a tree desirable to make one wise, she took of its fruit and ate. She also gave to her husband with her, and he ate. *Genesis 3:6*

11. Yes—referred to as Nephilim or giants. They are a non-human hybrid race created from procreation between the "sons of God" with human women.

1 When human beings began to increase in number on the earth and daughters were born to them, 2 the sons of God saw that the daughters of humans were beautiful, and they married any of them they chose...4 The Nephilim were on the earth in those days—and also afterward—when the sons of God went to the daughters of humans and had children by them. They were the heroes of old, men of renown. *Genesis 6:1-2, 4 (NIV)*

0 Then Caleb silenced the people before Moses and said, "We should go up and take possession of the land, for we can certainly do it." 31 But the men who had gone up with him said, "We can't attack those people; they are stronger than we are." 32 And they spread among the Israelites a bad report about the land they had explored. They said, "The land we explored devours those living in it. All the people

THE NO-HOMEWORK WOMEN'S BIBLE STUDY: GROUP HUG

we saw there are of great size. [33] We saw the Nephilim there (the descendants of Anak come from the Nephilim). We seemed like grasshoppers in our own eyes, and we looked the same to them."
Numbers 13:30-33

The Bible also talks about angels throughout its text. Technically, angels are non-human beings that live in another realm and visit earth, or aliens.

[6] And the angels who did not keep their positions of authority but abandoned their proper dwelling— these he has kept in darkness, bound with everlasting chains for judgment on the great Day.
Jude 1:6

In addition to angels existing as non-human creatures who live above the earth, a species of beings who live in the heavens called "watchers" are mentioned in the Bible:

[13] I saw in the visions of my head while on my bed, and there was a watcher, a holy one, coming down from heaven. *Daniel 4:13*

[17] This decision is by the decree of the watchers...
Daniel 4:17

[23] And inasmuch as the king saw a watcher, a holy one, coming down from heaven... *Daniel 4:23*

12. Jesus had many names: Jesus, Lord, Savior, Christ, Immanuel, Alpha and Omega, Bright and Morning Star, Good Shepherd, I Am, King of Kings, King of the Jews, Son of God, Lamb of God, Master, Prince of Life, Root of Jesse, Wonderful Counselor, Mighty God, Everlasting Father, Prince of Peace, Elohim, El Shaddai, El Roi, Jehovah-Jireh, Adonai, Coming King, Son of David.

WORKS CITED

WEEK 1

Image of Sleeping Dog: ID 82765475 © Noviantoko Tri Arijanto, Dreamstime.com.

Jones, Jeffrey M. "In US 40% Get Less Than Recommended Amount of Sleep." *Gallup*, Gallup, 19 December 2013, https://news.gallup.com/poll/166553/less-recommended-amount-sleep.aspx.

Thayer and Smith. "Greek Lexicon entry for Battologeo." *Strong's Exhaustive Concordance,* Salem Media Group, https://www.biblestudytools.com/lexicons/greek/kjv/battologeo.html.

Van Ness, Jonathan. "Jonathan Van Ness Quotes." *Brainy Quote*, https://www.brainyquote.com/authors/jonathan-van-ness-quotes.

WEEK 2

Greenwald, Morgan. "27 Genius Tips That Will Keep Your Home in Perfect Order." *Best Life*, Galvanized Media, 8 February 2019, https://bestlifeonline.com/home-organization-tips/.

Image of Disorganized Woman: ID 51245428 © Tigatelu, Dreamstime.com.

Thayer and Smith. "Greek Lexicon entry for Akatastasia." *Strong's Exhaustive Concordance,* Salem Media Group, https://www.biblestudytools.com/lexicons/greek/kjv/akatastasia.html.

Williamson, Maryanne. "Maryanne Williamson Quotes." *Brainy Quote*, https://www.brainyquote.com/authors/marianne-williamson-quotes.

WEEK 3

Cool Smarty. "Fact of the Day." *Cool Smarty*, Azrael Creatives, 3 February 2020, https://www.coolsmarty.com/2020/02/03/fact-of-the-day-609/.

Image of Narcissistic Turkey: ID 135500775 © Nicoleta Ionescu, Dreamstime.com.

Lincoln, Abraham. "Abraham Lincoln Quotes." *Brainy Quote*, https://www.brainyquote.com/quotes/abraham_lincoln_110340.

Thayer and Smith. "Greek Lexicon entry for Muthos." *Strong's Exhaustive Concordance,* Salem Media Group, https://www.biblestudytools.com/lexicons/greek/kjv/muthos.html.

WEEK 4
Image of Surprised Hamster: ID 92031788 © Refluo, Dreamstime.com.

Redlener, Irwin. "Irwin Redlener Quotes." *Brainy Quote*, https://www.brainyquote.com/authors/irwin-redlener-quotes.

Thayer and Smith. "Greek Lexicon entry for Ergon." *Strong's Exhaustive Concordance,* Salem Media Group, https://www.biblestudytools.com/lexicons/greek/kjv/ergon.html.

The Provident Living Guide to Family Preparedness. "Food Calculator." *Family Preparedness*, https://providentliving.com/preparedness/food-storage/foodcalc/.

WEEK 5
Boyles, Margaret. "Wondering About Oat Milk? Make Your Own!." *Farmer's Almanac*, Yankee Publishing, Inc., 3 February 2020, https://www.almanac.com/news/home-health/natural-living/wondering-about-oat-milk-make-your-own.

Image of Mouse with Weights: ID 139046287 © Sarah Holmlund, Dreamstime.com.

Somers, Suzanne. "Suzanne Somers Quotes." *Brainy Quote*, https://www.brainyquote.com/authors/suzanne-somers-quotes.

Thayer and Smith. "Greek Lexicon entry for Naos." *Strong's Exhaustive Concordance,* Salem Media Group, https://www.biblestudytools.com/lexicons/greek/kjv/naos.html.

WEEK 6

Image of Family: ID 45744227 © Tigatelu, Dreamstime.com.

My Southern Health. "10 Quick Tips for Improving Relationships." *Vanderbilt Health*, My Southern Health, 12 October 2017, https://www.mysouthernhealth.com/improve-relationship/.

Stanley, Charles. "Charles Stanley Quotes." *Brainy Quote*, https://www.brainyquote.com/authors/charles-stanley-quotes.

Thayer and Smith. "Greek Lexicon entry for Proton." *Strong's Exhaustive Concordance,* Salem Media Group, https://www.biblestudytools.com/lexicons/greek/kjv/proton.html.

WEEK 7

Aurelius, Marcus. "Marcus Aurelius Quotes." *Brainy Quote*, https://www.brainyquote.com/authors/marcus-aurelius-quotes.

Brown, Driver, Briggs, and Gesenius. "Hebrew Lexicon entry for Chayil." *Strong's Exhaustive Concordance*, Salem Media Group, https://www.biblestudytools.com/lexicons/hebrew/kjv/chayil.html.

Image of Professional Woman: ID 45741588 © Tigatelu, Dreamstime.com.

"Virtue." Collins Dictionary, *Collins.* https://www.collinsdictionary.com/dictionary/english/virtue.

WEEK 8

Fielding, Henry. "Henry Fielding Quotes." *Brainy Quote*, https://www.brainyquote.com/authors/henry-fielding-quotes.

Fry, Richard and Kochhar, Rakesh. "Are You in the Middle Class?" *Pew Research* Center, The Pew Charitable Trusts, 6 September 2018, https://www.pewresearch.org/fact-tank/2018/09/06/are-you-in-the-american-middle-class/.

Image of Squirrel with Nuts: ID 41949919 © Muhammad Desta Laksana, Dreamstime.com.

Thayer and Smith. "Greek Lexicon entry for Opheilo." *Strong's Exhaustive Concordance,* Salem Media Group, https://www.biblestudytools.com/lexicons/greek/kjv/opheilo.html.

WHAT DO YOU THINK?

Available at www.Amazon.com

ABOUT THE AUTHOR

Christine Tate, originally a Midwest native, grew up in the Northwest suburbs of Chicago. The only child of a successful floor trader and an Indiana farm girl, she was strongly influenced by conservative, "Bible Belt" Christian philosophies. She started college at the age of fifteen and graduated from USC with honors at nineteen earning a degree in Cinema-Television. After living on the West Coast for a number of years, Christine married the love of her life, Rick Tate. Christine went on to homeschool their daughter, Tabitha, while enjoying the travels and adventures of military life. During that time, she began writing Christian non-fiction.

Christine and her husband Rick currently live in Virginia Beach, VA where Rick retired from the Navy after a distinguished thirty-year career. Tabitha now attends a local High School where she enjoys her friends and activities. Christine is actively involved with church life and spends much of her time keeping up with family activities, producing the annual Virginia Beach Christian Readers and Authors Festival, mentoring other Christian authors, speaking at various events and writing Christian books. More information about the Christian Readers and Authors Festival can be found at https://christianauthorsfestival.webstarts.com. Information about new and upcoming releases from Christine Tate can be found at https://christinetate.webstarts.com.

Made in the USA
Monee, IL
24 May 2023